GET OUT OF DEBT (GOoD)

Quick, Fast, and in a Hurry!

DR. EVELYN Y. JENKINS

Copyright © 2014 Dr. Evelyn Y. Jenkins
All rights reserved
First Edition

PAGE PUBLISHING, INC.
New York, NY

First originally published by Page Publishing, Inc. 2014

ISBN 978-1-62838-928-9 (pbk)
ISBN 978-1-62838-929-6 (digital)

Printed in the United States of America

Contents

List of Tables and Figures 5
Disclaimer 7
Introduction 9

What Is Debt? 11
What Is Money? 13
Principles of Money Management 15
What's Keeping You in Debt? 17
Why Use GOoD Strategy? 23
How Does GOoD Work? 25
Phases of GOoD Strategy 31

Conclusion 35
Glossary 37
References 39
About the Author 40

List of Tables and Figures

Figure 1: Current Strategy 19

Table 1: GOoD Strategy Worksheet 27
Table 2: GOoD Tools 28

Figure 2: GOoD Strategy 31

Disclaimer

The methodology found in these pages are what personally worked for me, and I wanted to simplify what I have learned over the years in order to share with others who are currently faced with or who may become faced with a similar situation (drowning in debt). It is by no means the only method by which to eliminate debt. In my opinion, it is simply the most logical method that focuses on benefiting a borrower with the understanding that no two parties are the same. Therefore, the outcome will be determined based on personal diligence, income earned, amount of debt, and interest accrued.

Introduction

Are you drowning in debt? Does it often seem hopeless? Are you seeking another way to stop the bleeding other than foreclosure or filing bankruptcy? Well, if you answered yes to all three questions, then this guide is for you. However, the ideal situation would be to avoid debt at all cost, but if you find that this is impossible for you, then continue to read, and hopefully, you will walk away with the air needed to inflate your debt-elimination life raft.

In order to tackle debt, we must first understand it. Yes, I said understand it. This may seem crazy to some, but actually, it makes sense. In other words, do not get recognizing debt confused with understanding debt. Recognizing debt is when you know that you are in debt because you are receiving bills each month that indicates that you owe someone. Understanding debt is knowing how you got in debt, what the entities of debt are, and what your focus must become in order to eliminate the debt.

What Is Debt?

Debt is an obligation owed by one party, the *debtor,* to a second party, the *creditor*; usually, this refers to *assets* granted by the creditor to the debtor, but the term can also be used metaphorically to cover moral obligations and other interactions not based on economic value.

A debt is created when a creditor agrees to lend a sum of assets to a debtor. Debt is usually granted with expected repayment; in most cases, this includes repayment of the original sum, plus *interest*.

In the world of finance, debt is a means of using anticipated income and future purchasing power in the present before it has actually been earned, and I would like to also add that debt is closely affiliated with money management.

What Is Money?

Money is any object or record that is generally accepted as payment for goods and services and repayment of debts in a given socioeconomic context or country. It is also an asset, and if properly used, it can increase your net worth tremendously. One thing that we all must be aware of is that money is a magnet that can attract both positive and negative spirits. For example, money can assist you with bringing joy into one's life, if a person has the funds to take care of their personal needs or to handle unexpected emergencies. In other words, money can be used to do many good things. Galatians 5:22–23 states that the fruit of the Spirit is love, joy, peace, forbearance, kindness, goodness, faithfulness, gentleness, and self-control. Against such things there is no law. Therefore, the premise is that if you were to use money to promote these things, there is no limit as to what can be done.

On the other hand, if a person lacks self-control (the spirit of the flesh) when dealing with money, it can manifest worry, sadness, or depression. For the flesh desires what is contrary to the Spirit, and the Spirit what is contrary to the flesh. They are in conflict with each other (Galatians 5:17). The acts of the flesh are obvious: sexual immorality, impurity and debauchery, idolatry and witchcraft, hatred, discord, jealousy, fits of rage, selfish ambition, dissensions, factions and envy, drunkenness, orgies, and the like (Galatians 5:19–21).

The O'Jays described it best in 1973 when they wrote the song For the Love of Money. The lyrics clearly states what can happen when money is mismanaged or is used for illicit purposes. For example:

- Some people will steal from their mother
- Some people will rob their own brother

GET OUT OF DEBT (GOOD)

- Some people won't care who they hurt or beat
- A woman will sell her precious body

In other words, money can drive some people out of their minds; it will sometimes change you. However, the O'Jays go on to say that people should not let money rule them; instead, we should do good things with it.

Hint: Walk by the Spirit, and you will not gratify the desires of the flesh…for those who belong to Christ have crucified the flesh with its passions and desires (Galatians 5:16, 24)

Principles of Money Management

Principle 1: Only use credit cards for their intended purpose. Simply stated, do not use credit cards unless you can pay them off on or prior to the due date. Zero debt is always better than thousands.

Exception: Not unless you are using OPM—also known as other people's money—to enhance your overall money management plan and provided you are walking with the spirit of self-control.

Principle 2: Always pay yourself. In other words, plan for the future. The question is not "if" something unexpected will happen, the question is "when" the unexpected happens, will you be ready? If you make an effort to pay others on time, then you should also make an effort to pay yourself. After all, you and your family are just as important.

Principle 3: Stop practicing insanity. Albert Einstein stated that "insanity is doing the same thing over and over again and expecting different results." Do not get caught on that rat wheel. Do something different. If it did not work in the past, then it will not work in the future.

Principle 4: Stop taking advice from bootleg advisors. Taking advice from those who are worse off than you are or who have no proven track record will only put you in the same sinking ship that they are in. Seek someone out who has achieved what you would like to achieve, and ask them to show you how they did what they did. In most cases, what you will find is that they are more than willing to help. The only reason they had not shared their knowledge in

GET OUT OF DEBT (GOOD)

the past is that they needed permission by you to enter your space. Better yet, seek out a professional.

What's Keeping You in Debt?

There are numerous excuses as to why people are in debt, but the belief is that there are only two legitimate reasons, and they are: behavior and annual percentage rates/yields.

Behavior

Our behavior is what will often get us into trouble with regards to debt. Normally, there are four things that will occur. Failure to use credit cards for their intended purpose; failure to plan for the future; the methodology used to pay off debt; and failure to talk to others who can help.

FAILURE TO USE CREDIT CARDS FOR INTENDED PURPOSE

Credit cards should be used to take advantage of certain things that cannot be done through other means. For example, in order to take advantage of acquiring "no interest" deals for a period of time (1, 3, 6, or 12 months). Another example would be to secure rental cars because this is the means by which rental car companies have chosen to conduct business. Credit cards can also be used to receive discounts (10 percent, 20 percent, etc.) on purchases that you would not receive had you paid cash. These are all legitimate reasons for using a credit card, but should only be done if you have the funds to pay the entire bill off on or prior to its due date.

Hint: I hope you noticed that *I did not mention* that credit cards are to be used to buy new dresses, shoes, or man toys on a weekly basis to make us feel better or to keep up with the proverbial Joneses. "Let us not become conceited…and envying each other" (Galatians 5:26).

If you are shopping every week to receive gratification, then that may be a sign of depression, and you probably should seek help elsewhere.

FAILURE TO PLAN FOR THE FUTURE

We often find ourselves in debt because we have failed to plan for the future. In other words, when a crisis occurs that often requires funding, we will, more often than not, rely on the credit card(s) that we are carrying around in our pockets. We do this because we have failed to plan for the future. In other words, savings are nonexistent. As a result, we may max out the credit cards to meet the emergency need. However, by doing this, it will often overextend our budgets, if we have one. It also extends the inevitable—the inability to pay the entire bill off on or prior to its due date.

METHODOLOGY USED TO PAY DEBT

The way we pay debt keeps us in debt. We have always been taught that once we get paid, we are to pay our bills at the beginning of the month or on the bill's due date. Once the bills have been paid, then we can spend the remainder on whatever we choose. Therefore, more often than not, we go shopping to buy things that we do not need and cannot afford. In short, we accumulate more bills that may affect how we pay future obligations. See current methodology in figure 1. Most times, we are not taught that we should avoid this type of behavior and that we should focus on attacking APR or APY if we find ourselves in debt. APR is similar to APY, but it does not take compounding interest into account.

WHAT'S KEEPING YOU IN DEBT?

In other words, APR is a simpler way of handling interest. We are taught, as long as you are not late in paying debt, you are fine; however, whether you are late or not, interest accrual does not sleep nor does it take a break, it continues. The idea that lower interest rates benefits the borrower is somewhat true, but there is no better interest rate than 0 percent interest. This (lower interest) is what has become known as the "Jedi mind trick". You are made to believe that what you are doing is beneficial to you when it is only benefiting the recipient. The reality is that interest continues to accrue not unless you use a methodology that will decrease the APR/APY substantially. In other words, use a methodology that will keep the interest from overtaking or exceeding your input. Yes, by paying the debt the traditional way, you will eventually pay that bill off, but not before you give the lender their slice of the pie that is normally an exorbitant amount over and above the original amount of the loan.

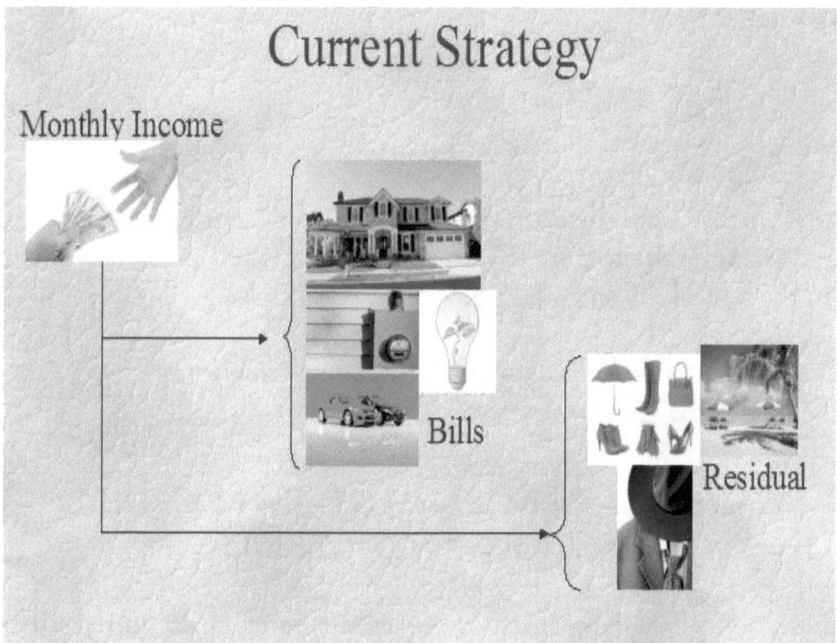

Figure 1: Current Strategy

FAILURE TO TALK TO OTHERS WHO CAN HELP

When we find ourselves approaching financial ruin, we often will not reach out for assistance until it is too late. The sad truth of the matter is that we know that dooms day is around the corner. We just decide to ignore it, bury our heads in the sand, or avoid talking about it; hoping that it will eventually go away, but it will not. It will be there each and every day that we wake up until we decide to do something about it. We will many times "keep it to ourselves" as though we are going to come up with some bright idea for getting out of debt.

If that were the case, many of you would not be reading this guide. After all, you are the one who put yourself in this position in the first place, so go figure.

Hint: Pride goes before destruction, a haughty spirit before a fall (Proverbs 16:18).

ANNUAL PERCENTAGE RATE/YIELD (APR) AND (APY)

Now, once we have used those credit cards or acquired that debt through some form of contract, we will often have annual percentage rate (APR) or annual percentage yield (APY) to deal with, if we did not pay the entire bill off on or prior to its due date.

APR is similar to APY, but it does not take compounding into account. It is a simpler way of handling interest. The downfall for the borrower is that knowing APR does not give the borrower an accurate account of what is truly owed. There lies the problem. Since most debt accrue interest in a manner that is similar to the way that credit cards and mortgages accrue interest, let's look at the difference between credit cards and mortgages.

With credit cards, APR tells you what interest rate you pay, but it does not include the effects of compounding; so in reality, you probably pay more than the APR. If you only make small payments on your credit card, you will start paying interest not only on the money you borrowed, but *you will also pay interest on the interest that was previously charged to you.* This compounding effect can raise your cost of borrowing higher than you might think. Instead of looking at the APR, APY would be a more accurate description of how much you pay.

In addition, APR for credit cards only includes interest costs, it doesn't account for the other fees you pay to your credit card company, so you have to research and compare those costs separately. Annual fees, balance transfer fees, and other charges can add up, so a card with a slightly higher APR might be better in some cases (depending on how you use your card). In addition, your credit card might have several different APRs, so you pay different rates for different types of transactions (e.g., cash advances versus purchases).

With mortgage loans, APR is complicated because it *does* include more than just your interest charges. Any quotes you get may or may not include closing costs that you will have to pay or other payments required to get your loan approved (such as private mortgage insurance). Lenders have the ability to choose whether or not certain items are part of the APR calculation, so you have to look closely if you are comparing loans.

GET OUT OF DEBT (GOOD)

In summary, credit card loans are a good example of the importance of understanding APR versus APY. If you carry a balance, you pay an APY that is higher than the quoted APR. Why? Because interest charges are added to your balance each month, and in the following month, you will have to pay interest *on top of that interest* (this is similar to earning interest on top of interest you have earned in a savings account). The difference might not be huge, but there is a difference. The larger your loan and the longer you borrow, the bigger that difference becomes.

With a fixed rate mortgage, on the other hand, APR is accurate because you will not add interest charges and increase your loan balance, not unless your payments are late.

Hint: APY is more accurate than APR in some situations (because it tells you what a loan *really* costs); unfortunately, when you borrow money, you typically only hear about the APR. In reality, you might actually pay APY, which is almost always higher with certain types of loans.

Why Use GOoD Strategy?

You may ask yourself, why use GOoD strategy? I am here to tell you that the answer is relatively simple, it works.

For example, let's say that you are $100,000 in debt, and you would like to pay it off. The interest on the debt is 7 percent. Your payments are around $665 per month. Under normal circumstances or the normal way of paying off debt at that rate, it may take you approximately 30 years to pay off that amount of debt. However, if you were to use the GOoD strategy for paying that same amount of debt it would take you approximately 2 years and 1 month, saving you $132,057 in interest payments, and allowing you to put money in your pocket faster.

How Does GOoD Work?

Now that we understand what debt is and how we got into this mess in the first place, we must now take steps to eliminate the debt. So the question becomes, what do we do about it? Let's say that you have two bills—one for $50,000 and the other for $100,000—which one could you pay off faster? Of course, it is the one for $50,000.

The key is that you can pay off a small bill faster than you can pay off a large one. Also, the small funding source can be used as an extension to your monthly income vice as a means by which to go shopping for things that you do not need. Knowing this fact, you can use the small sum of funding, which is larger than your average paycheck, to make a substantial impact on the bill that you would like to eliminate.

It does not matter what type of debt you have—small or large, car, home, credit cards, etc. The good news is that this process can be used to eliminate any interest accruing debt, if followed as directed. In addition, this methodology for paying debt does not require a lifestyle change . Yes, you got it right. This methodology does not require a lifestyle change. However, the first thing that must be realized is that a change in behavior is required. As previously stated, our behavior is what will often get us into trouble with regards to debt. Therefore, it is our behavior that will help to get us out of debt. The second thing that must be understood is that to attack APR and/or APY is to attack the debt. If you understand those two things, then let's get started.

In this section, you will find another legitimate way to use credit; so, pay close attention as we go through the steps required to eliminate the debt.

GET OUT OF DEBT (GOOD)

Step 1: Determine Expenses and Income

Step 1 requires that you know your exact input and output.

- Determine your monthly expenses to include all bills, vacations, and entertainment (do not leave anything out, including what you put into savings each month). Again, *pay yourself.* For all bills, you must identify monthly amounts due as well as the balance owed. Bills also include mortgage and/or rent. See table 1, columns 3 and 4.

- Determine your monthly income (from all sources). See table 1, column 1.

Step 2: Identify Source

Step 2 involves identifying the source that will assist you with getting out of debt, the target or debt that you would like to obliterate, and the strategy needed to accomplish this feat.

- Source—To be most effective, your source must equal, at a minimum, to a three-month salary. Your source will assist you with getting out of debt and can come from various means. For example, your source can come from a tax refund, part time income, use of other people's money or OPM (friend, family, line of credit, or credit card), or you may borrower from yourself (401[k] or savings). See table 1, column 2. Using these means will allow you to set up what will become known as your *source account.* A source account will be used strictly to pay your target and monthly bills. If you are using a particular credit card or line of credit exclusively for this purpose, then the credit card or line of credit used becomes your source account. If you are using cash, 401(k) or savings, then the bank account where payments are deducted each month becomes the source account.

- Target—Your target or the debt that you would like to eliminate must be identified, and you must know the monthly payments that are due as well as the balance owed. For example, your target could be a car note, house note, credit card(s), line of credit, or all of the previously mentioned combined. See table 1, column 5 and table 2. Column 5 reflects the GOoD Strategy. However, based on an analysis that was conducted in 2014, the numbers shown to the right of Column 5 reflect the month and year that it would take an average individual to arrive at that same financial point in time if they were to use the traditional method of paying debt.

GET OUT OF DEBT (GOOD)

Table 1: GOoD Strategy Worksheet

Monthly	Input/Output		Residual	Source			Total Expenses		Monthly Expenses		Target	
	Income	Output										$100,000.00
1	$ 5,000.00	$ 1,000.00	$ 4,000.00	Tax Refund	Friend/Family	$ 15,000.00	Mortgage/Rent	$ 50,000.00	Mortgage/Rent	500	Feb-24	$ 14,000.00 / $ 86,000.00
2	$ 5,000.00	$ 1,000.00	$ 4,000.00	Part Time			Bills	$ 35,000.00	Bills	200		$ 1,000.00 / $ 85,000.00
3	$ 5,000.00	$ 1,000.00	$ 4,000.00	OPM	LOC	$ 11,000.00	Entertainment	$ 15,000.00	Entertainment	300		$ 1,000.00 / $ 84,000.00
4	$ 5,000.00	$ 1,000.00	$ 4,000.00		CC	$ 7,000.00	Total	$ 100,000.00	Total	1000		$ 1,000.00 / $ 83,000.00
5	$ 5,000.00	$ 1,000.00	$ 4,000.00	Borrow/Self	401K/Savings $ 15,000.00	$ 3,000.00					Mar-31	$ 1,000.00 / $ 82,000.00
6	$ 5,000.00	$ 1,000.00	$ 4,000.00	Windfall		$ (1,000.00)						$ 14,000.00 / $ 68,000.00
7	$ 5,000.00	$ 1,000.00	$ 4,000.00	Total								$ 1,000.00 / $ 67,000.00
8	$ 5,000.00	$ 1,000.00	$ 4,000.00									$ 1,000.00 / $ 66,000.00
9	$ 5,000.00	$ 1,000.00	$ 4,000.00	Interest							Dec-35	$ 1,000.00 / $ 65,000.00
10	$ 5,000.00	$ 1,000.00	$ 4,000.00	Payor	$139,511							$ 14,000.00 / $ 64,000.00
11	$ 5,000.00	$ 1,000.00	$ 4,000.00	Save	$132,057							$ 1,000.00 / $ 50,000.00
12	$ 5,000.00	$ 1,000.00	$ 4,000.00	2 Years	$14,489							$ 1,000.00 / $ 49,000.00
												$ 1,000.00 / $ 48,000.00
											Jun-39	$ 14,000.00 / $ 47,000.00
												$ 1,000.00 / $ 46,000.00
												$ 1,000.00 / $ 32,000.00
												$ 1,000.00 / $ 31,000.00
												$ 14,000.00 / $ 30,000.00
												$ 1,000.00 / $ 29,000.00
											Apr-42	$ 1,000.00 / $ 28,000.00
												$ 14,000.00 / $ 14,000.00

STEP 3: IDENTIFY STRATEGY

Step 3 involves identifying the sequence of events that should occur to eliminate the debt by attacking the APR/APY.

- Strategy—Your strategy will indicate the sequence of events (when to pay bills, when to increase the payment to the target, and when to repay your source).

Table 2 gives you a quick reference that includes source, target, and strategy.

Table 2: GOoD Tools

Potential Source(s)	Potential Target(s)	Strategy
Tax refund	Home	Phase I. Take lump sum funds from source account (three-month salary), minus monthly bill amount, and apply to target and monthly bills respectively.
Part-time income	Car	Phase II. Repay source account using all monthly income.

GET OUT OF DEBT (GOOD)

OPM Friend/family Line of credit Credit cards	Credit cards	Phase III. Pay all monthly bills from source account.
Borrow from self 401(k) Savings		Repeat phases II and III until source balance is zero if credit card or line of credit is used as source account or until balance equals the original amount that you started with if cash, savings, or 401(k) is used.
Windfall (unexpected influx of money)	Line of credit	When the source account reaches its original state, repeat phase I. Continue through the process, repeating phases II and III until the desired target (bill) balance is zero.

Phases of GOoD Strategy

- Phase I—Take lump sum funds from source account (three-month salary), minus monthly bill amount, and apply to target and monthly bills respectively.
- Phase II—Repay source account using all monthly income.
- Phase III—Pay all monthly bills from source account.
- Repeat Phases II and III until source balance is zero if credit card or line of credit is used as source account or until balance equals the original amount that you started with if cash, savings, or 401(k) is used. See figure 2.
- When the source account reaches its original state, repeat phase I. Continue through the process, repeating phases II and III until the desired target (bill) balance is zero.

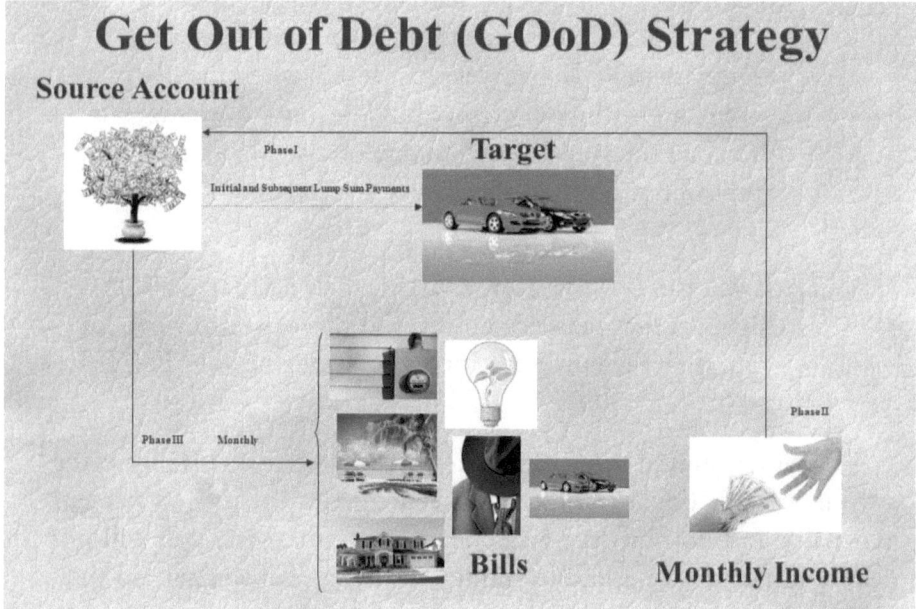

Figure 2: GOoD Strategy

GET OUT OF DEBT (GOOD)

Now that you have had the opportunity to review both the debt-elimination tools and process flow, you may be wondering how do you get started if you don't have the money already, if you do not have a credit card or line of credit to pull from, or friends to call on? Well, that's why I wrote the guide. So let me help you with that.

If you do not have the funds needed to begin your debt-elimination program, the recommendation would be to do one of the following:

1. If you can use OPM, then do that; and since we know that money is an asset, regardless of whose money it is (yours or OPM), you can use it to your benefit to eliminate debt. In other words, this is when the use of a credit card or line of credit could become advantageous provided the spirit of self-control is also practiced; but if you can not do that, then move to recommendation 2.

2. If you can borrow from yourself, then do that. This is highly recommended; however, if this does not work for you, then recommendations 3 or 4 may be your best bet.

Note: Should you decide to borrow from yourself by using your 401(k), do not authorize the deduction of the 10 percent penalty and do not have taxes taken out; otherwise, you will not have the amount needed to fulfill your need. Yes, you can do that, so do not allow anyone to tell you otherwise. However, if they insist on taking the taxes and penalty out, then you may want to

PHASES OF GOOD STRATEGY

think of moving your funds to a self-directed IRA or to an account elsewhere where you will be given this option. This is another Jedi mind trick. Some organizations may not want you to take the money out because it does not benefit them. Therefore, you will be made to think that this is the worst thing that you can possibly do, and it is for them, but not for you. It is your money, and you should be given the option to pay the IRS up front when you remove the funds or to pay them on the back end at tax time. So with that being said, you will want to do this within the first three months of a new year so that it will allow you the time needed to replace what was borrowed by tax time of the following year. Better yet, this will also allow you to use your money without paying the penalty or the taxes.

3. At bare minimum, you could begin saving a little to acquire the three-month salary to get started.
4. You could also get a part-time job long enough to save for a three-month salary. This should be the amount of your regular salary, not part-time salary.

Now, you are ready to begin.

GET OUT OF DEBT (GOOD)

Conclusion

What have we learned? We have learned that debt is an obligation owed by one party, the *debtor*, to a second party, the creditor; and that it is closely affiliated with money management. We have learned that the management of money attracts both positive and negative spirits. Therefore, how you manage your money will determine the spirits that follow you around. For the most part, we have learned that what keeps us in debt is our behavior and whether or not the debt comes with annual percentage rate/yields. We have also learned that there are principles to managing money. And finally, we have found that the good news is that there is a methodology that can help us to get out of debt quick, fast, and in a hurry. This can be done by determining our expenses and income, identifying the source that will help us to catapult our money management plan, and by becoming familiar with the strategy needed to get us through the debt-elimination process.

Now you have it—there is life after debt. Once you have gone through this debt-elimination process, you will never look at debt the same way. So I will see you on the other side of that mountain of debt, and for some of you, once you have eliminated the debt, I will look forward to assisting you with getting your credit straight.

Glossary

Annual Percentage Rate. Otherwise known as APR. Annual percentage rate (APR) is a tool for understanding the cost of a loan in terms of percentage, whether it's a credit card or a mortgage.

Annual Percentage Yield. Otherwise known as APY. Annual percentage yield is the return on an investment over the course of a year. If you are the *investor*, it refers to your earnings or how much money you're making. If, on the other hand, you are the *borrower*, it refers to the lender's return or how much you pay them in interest (and possibly fees).

Asset. In financial accounting, an *asset* is an economic resource. Anything tangible or intangible that is capable of being owned or controlled to produce value and that is held to have positive economic value is considered an asset. Simply stated, assets represent value of ownership that can be converted into cash.

Debt. A *debt* is an obligation owed by one party, the *debtor,* to a second party, the *creditor*. Usually, this refers to *assets* granted by the creditor to the debtor, but the term can also be used metaphorically to cover moral obligations and other interactions not based on economic value.

Creditor. A person, bank, or company that lends money to someone; one to whom a debt is owed; *especially,* a person to whom money or goods are due.

Debtor. A person, organization, government, etc. that owes money; one guilty of neglect or violation of duty.

Interest. A charge for borrowed money; generally a percentage of the amount borrowed; the profit in goods or money that is made on invested capital; an excess above what is due or expected.

Jedi mind trick. When a person is made to believe that what they are doing is beneficial to them, when in reality it is only benefiting the recipient or those who have interest in profiting from that person's actions.

Money. Money is any object or record that is generally accepted as payment for goods and services and repayment of debts in a given socioeconomic context or country; an asset; a magnet.

OPM. Otherwise known as other people's money; money borrowed from friend, family, or institution (i.e., bank, credit card, finance, or mortgage company).

Source. A source assists a person with getting out of debt and can come from various means (i.e., tax refund, part time income, use of other people's money or OPM, or from the person's personal 401[k] or savings).

Source account. A source account is a credit card, line of credit, or bank account dedicated to paying target and monthly bills.

Target. The debt or bill that a person would like to eliminate or pay off.

REFERENCES

Albert Einstein, (n.d.)., *BrainyQuote.com*, accessed March 10, 2014, http://www.brainyquote.com/quotes/quotes/a/alberteins133991.html

Jeremy Vohwinkle, *The Difference Between APR and APY*, accessed March 10, 2014, http://financialplan.about.com/od/savingmoney/qt/APRvsAPY.htm

Jerry Sterner and Alvin Sargent, Canadian Film Centre, Toronto, Canada: *Other People's Money*, 1991.

Justin Pritchard, *Annual Percentage Yield-APY: Learning, Earning, and Calculating APY*, accessed March 10, 2014, http://banking.about.com/od/savings/a/apy.htm

O'Jays, *Ship Ahoy: For the Love of Money*, 1973.

Thomas Nelson, Thomas Nelson, Inc: *The Holy Bible: KJV*, 2004.

T.J. Marrs, *Living Free and Clear Debt Elimination Wealth Building System*, 2014.

Wikimedia Foundation, Inc., Encyclopedia: *Wikipedia*, accessed February 4, 2014, http://en.wikipedia.org/wiki/Debt

About the Author

Dr. Evelyn Yvonne Jenkins, the daughter of Evelyn Odessa Cobb and Philip Jenkins, is a native of Brunswick, Georgia, and currently resides in Clinton, Maryland, a part of the Washington, DC, metropolitan area. She is an alumna of the Regent University in Virginia Beach, Virginia, where she achieved her Doctorate of Philosophy, specializing in the study of Organizational Leadership. She is the CEO of her own company called Jenkins & Associates Consulting LLC, which provides services to the federal government in business consulting. She also provides services in the renovation of real estate, debt elimination, and energy conservation. In her spare time, she sits on the board of directors of a company called Applied Computing Technologies Inc. in Springfield, Virginia, and chairs Prince George's County National Congress of Black Women Inc., a nonprofit organization. She is a flutist in the Ebenezer African Methodist Episcopal Church Orchestra in Fort Washington, Maryland, where she attends church regularly; and prior to that, she served twenty-five years in the United States Navy, retiring as a Master Chief (E9) Personnelman.